365
Perfect Things
to Say to
Your Kids

Maureen Healy

365
Perfect Things
to Say to
Your Kids

Growing Happy Kids, LLC

Published in the United States by Growing Happy Kids, LLC
First edition published 2010.
Growing Happy Kids is a registered trademark.

Visit us at www.growinghappykids.com

For information regarding bulk purchases, please contact Small Press United (IPG) at 1-800-888-4741.

Cover Design: Kory Bailey
Interior Layout: Kara Brown
Editorial Consultant: Jonna Rae Bartges
Design Consultant: Trish Healy

Library of Congress Control Number: 2009911277

ISBN-13   978-0-6153-2390-9

ISBN-10   0-6153-2390-1

Printed in the United States of America.

Note
The intent of the author is only to offer information of a general nature to assist you in communicating with your child. In the event you use any of the information contained in this book, which is your constitutional right, the author and the publisher assume no responsibility for your actions.

365 Perfect Things to Say to Your Kids
by
Maureen Healy

Contents

Gratitude

Introduction   1

Section I: Empowering   9

Section II: Educating   45

Section III: Inspiring   83

Resources

About the Author

Dedication

Gratitude

Thank you to my teachers who tirelessly (and often without pay) worked to train my mind and heart.

A special note of thanks also goes to my child clients and all the children around the world – you serve as a constant source of love, inspiration and joy for me each day. Keep telling me about your lives.

I also have a deep well of gratitude for you, the awakened adult, who commits to bring out the best in children. Without you, none of my dreams are possible. And with you, it's all possible – we can change the world!

Acknowledgements

I want to acknowledge all of my colleagues who read an advance copy of this book. A special note of recognition goes to Judith Orloff, Kathy Eldon and Ray Hawkins for their empowering words.

I also want to acknowledge and remember my parents, Joseph and Margaret Healy.

Introduction

Sayings

Whatever words we utter should be chosen with care for people will hear them and be influenced by them for good or ill.

Buddha

Words have wounded us and healed our hearts. They have empowered us or dashed our dreams. Lives have been lost and saved over simple sayings. The power of words is impossible to fully understand, and no one is more influenced by words than a growing child.

Children feel and experience this world so deeply. Listening to our words is a powerful part of their growing story. Every child begins to see him or her self through the words of an adult. It is such words that begin to shape a child's sense of worth, and often influences the path of their life.

Being able to harness the power of words, I believe, is an essential component of positive parenting. It is parenting with awareness. Every word spoken to your child has the awesome ability to pave a positive pathway in his or her brain. Words or sayings needn't be perfect but ideally are spoken with great enthusiasm, meaning and repetition so they become a true force for good.

And since children are developing at such an incredibly rapid pace – every word counts!

Consider Austin, age 3, who still talks to me about his friend calling him stupid. It rocked him to his core. Or Amy, age 6, who smiled ear-to-ear when her mother praised her painted plate. It fully encouraged Amy's creativity! Or Kai, age 11, who cried after his father said, "Guess, we don't have Picasso here!" His Dad surely didn't intend to squelch the boy's lifelong creativity but those weren't the right words.

Saying the right words isn't always easy. It takes a bit of awareness. It doesn't necessarily come naturally. The good news is that everyone can learn how to use words as powerful tools to propel their child's best life.

East meets West

I was born with what Einstein calls a "holy curiosity" regarding the mind. My favorite word was "why" as a child. Always did I seek to understand why people did certain things, how they thought and find the causal connections. Needless to say "why" got old with my mother quickly, and her reply soon became "Because I said so!" I wasn't deterred.

Endlessly fascinated, I later pursued degrees in both psychology as well as clinical psychology. "Why" was still beating in my heart, it was alive in me. Soon I found myself working directly with kids on topics of emotional health, diagnosing as well as treating them within the paradigm of clinical psychology. Good news is that I was beginning to crack some of my "why" questions but as usual they led to more unanswerable questions…

And that is where Tibetan Buddhism emerged on my path. I wanted to end suffering in myself as well as others. Psychology, for me, was a temporary band-aid to alleviate pain but not really cause its cessation. And the new age movement with its vast array of leading-edge teachers was helpful but not the panacea. So one thing led to another, and I have had the great fortune of being a student to Tibetan Masters. As well as being a teacher alongside extraordinary Tibetan scholars as we educated kids.

So I share my path for two reasons. First, the sayings in this book are informed by complex child development theories and my professional experience nurturing the formation of child's self-concept, worldview and health, no matter how whimsical or unassuming they appear. Second, such words were also greatly influenced by Tibetan Buddhism. Buddhism centers upon cultivating compassion, kindness, joy, love, patience, interconnectedness, equanimity, generosity, and happiness.

So all of this is my offering to you. A book of sayings that draws upon the best of Eastern and Western thinking to empower, educate and inspire your child.

Parenting: Made Easier

Parenting has become a juggling act of unforeseen proportions. There always seems to be a new extracurricular activity for your child, your work requires more time and travel, your parents may be aging, costs are skyrocketing, your babysitter moved and your dog died. It all happens at once, leaving little time to craft just the "right" words to influence a child's positive growth.

That's why *365 Perfect Things to Say to Your Kids* was crafted. It provides you, the busy parent, with ready-made sayings to grow a happy child.

As well as I believe more parents are focused upon their children's happiness. Gone are the days where parents solely wanted their children to get "good jobs" but now we want them to have rewarding lives! Our aim has shifted. We have entered the age of Authentic Parenting. Parenting from the heart.

Such a task requires honesty and clear communication. It begins with literally meaning the words you say and saying the words you mean. It is empowering. It is partnering with your child on this great big journey we call life. It is not about controlling your child, but cultivating him or her.

Parents, educators and adults alike remain "in charge," but more as a coach along this path. We are really in it together. Each of us is growing, learning, teaching and becoming more authentic, empowered, skilled and inspired to live our dreams on this planet. Such a shift in raising our children has the potency to transform the world.

And your words are a powerful part of that equation. I believe it really is as Shakespeare stated, "The voice of parents is the voice of gods, for to their children they are heaven's lieutenants." So to make this incredibly influential role a little bit easier, the sayings in this book are presented.

Kid's Gain

Every saying in this book was designed to empower your child. I want your child to learn early on that anything is possible, and dreams really do come true! And to feel in every cell of their being that life is to be enjoyed, explored, discovered and savored as they become more. Coupled with this positive energy are analytical teachings upon multiple subjects such as integrity, honesty and equanimity.

So kid's gain by getting playful and purposeful affirmations that empower them. Every section has a very specific aim to cultivate key internal qualities that strengthen, inform and inspire your child. Specifically:

> **Section I**   In the **Empowering** chapter, your child gains: Courage, Confidence, Optimism, Connection and Self-Trust.

> **Section II**   In the **Educating** chapter, your child learns about: Emotional Awareness, Social and Service Learning, Ethical Living and Universal Truths.

> **Section III**   In the **Inspiring** chapter, your child connects with his or her: Inspiration, Imagination, Creativity, Love of Nature, Art and Spirit.

Each section also plays a key role in formulating a child's understanding of themselves as well as their view of the world. More specifically:

- ♦ *Empowering* sayings were crafted to support the formation of a **positive self-concept**.

- ♦ *Educating* sayings were crafted to support the formation of a **skillful worldview**. It is one that helps him or her self as well as others.

- ♦ *Inspiring* sayings were crafted to spark a **creative connection** to something Greater (i.e. Art, Spirit, Nature etc...).

Such seemingly simple psychological handiwork has been brewing in me for years. As I believe with all my heart there is no more worthy aim than bringing out the best in kids!

How To Use This Book

Make the sayings in this book your own. *Enjoy delving into their concepts, simplicity and power.* Mark the ones that seem to really "click" for you and your child.

Such sayings, when repeated with emotion and conviction, will create a positive force for good. Each will plant a seed. With continual encouragement and dialogue with your child, he or she will begin to internalize these concepts, feel their power and create their world with them. So practically speaking, my suggestions are as follows:

♦ **Make a Ritual** – Perhaps lock in a time everyday or every week that you designate as "Saying Time." You then read one of the sayings to your child. This quick, little bonding ritual becomes fun and something he or she happily anticipates.

♦ **Conversation Starters** – You may select a saying as a bouncing off point. You begin by reading a saying, and then expand on the concept by discussing it with your child. Any of the sayings easily becomes a conversation starter.

♦ **Create a Book** – Encourage your child to write down his or her favorite sayings in a journal as he or she begins collecting, illustrating and imagining them! Your child can then add sayings of his or her own creation.

♦ **Pick a Saying** – Allow your child to randomly pick a saying from the book. It encourages this process to be playful and practical. You may also enjoy how sychronistically the saying choosen appears to be just the right one, at just the right time!

♦ **Circle Time** – Use this book as an educational tool if you are leading a group of children in a classroom or group setting. Pick a saying to illustrate or discuss, thereby building the emotional, mental and spiritual health of all the children.

All and all, properly using this book needs to be fun. Creative ways to make such sayings fun is endless. One more idea is to pick numbers out of a hat that correspond to sayings. The possibilities go on and on. The point is that sharing such positive and powerful affirmations between you and your child can be a delightful adventure!

Some of these sayings also tackle big concepts – impermenance, honesty, interconnectedness, happiness and emotional health. Be sure to take time with these powerful topics. You can still have fun with them, but at the same time recognize their potential depth and breadth.

One More Piece

Sayings contained in this book are one piece of a larger mosaic of how to raise a happy child. They are not everything. They have their limitations. They also have their power.

Words, to me, are one of the most powerful pieces of growing a happy child. It is the words of love, hatred, joy, misery, happiness or hope that begin to propel a child. A child's world is largely kinesthetic, while words seem to heighten what the child is feeling. Adults have the opportunity to mirror their positive feelings via words towards a child, and help them on their journey towards unconditional self-acceptance, confidence and courageous faith.

Every child needs your support in mustering the courage to pursue his or her best life! In today's world we need everyones best, with their talents put to good use.

Section Key

Empowering

Educating

Inspiring

Section I
Empowering

The educator must believe in the potential power of his pupil, and he must employ all of his art in seeking to bring his pupil to experience this power.

Alfred Adler

Empower
literally means to "put in" or "to cause" power as derived from its Latin roots.

Empowering children
is a process of instilling them with beliefs and feelings that they are powerful now, as well as creating optimum conditions that mirror back to them these concepts.

Empowering our children is essential. It gives them the courage, faith and confidence to incarnate their best lives. The act of empowering doesn't diminish your power, but rather infuses it into the life force of your child. As more and more children accept and own their abilities, this world will be transformed. Talents unimagined will emerge to solve age-old dilemmas.

Invisible Acts

The act of empowering another is mostly invisible. Such invisible forces are utilized to shape a child's very visible world (i.e. behavior). Such efforts include the development of key internal qualities such as:

- ◆ Courage
- ◆ Confidence
- ◆ Self-trust
- ◆ Optimism
- ◆ Connection

All of the above internal qualities add power to a child's growing system. Each is important. Together they influence the creation of a **positive self-concept** that fuels a child's growth and potential in this world.

Empowering Kids: The 5 Key Qualities

Every child wants to feel strong, powerful and capable of doing anything in this world. Instead of socializing this quality out of them, this section's sayings encourage that boundless spirit via nurturing the qualities of courage, confidence, self-trust, optimism and connection.

Courage
: An ability to be strong from the inside out. A child with courage faces life's unknown situations with bravery and inner strength.

Confidence
: An ability to extend belief in oneself. A confident child believes that he or she *can* do it, and win the spelling bee!

Self-trust
: An ability to extend faith in oneself. A child displaying self-trust seeks to express his or her own unique creative expression. Johnny made a one-of-a-kind birdhouse with a skylight, and antennae. He trusted his instincts.

Optimism
: An ability to look at the positive side of life. A child that is optimistic learns to look for the opportunity and possibility in most events (i.e. how to make lemonade from lemons).

Connection
: An ability to relate to self and others. Susie, age 3, learned how to interact with other children, valuing them and respecting their space.

Such qualities above, I assure you, can be cultivated. That is the great news! So enjoy taking the focused time to select a saying that speaks to you, and nurtures one of these ever-important aspects in your child.

Tips

- **S**et aside your own emotional and mental "baggage" at the door.

- **G**et into a positive state of mind *(Take a few deep belly breaths or focus on feeling gratitude).*

- **F**ocus unerringly on "building your child up" to believe: Anything is Possible, You Can Do It and The World Will Support You.

- **S**elect a saying that speaks to you right here, right now.

- **R**emember it is the *quality,* not quantity, of your time together that counts!

Empowering Sayings

1
Celebrate Who You Are

You are perfect right now! Let's celebrate who you ARE as a rising star. You shine like the sun and glow like the moon. You ARE strong like a tree and vast like the sea. You are such a great gift to me.

2
Trust Your Feelings

Let your feelings point the way. Happy ones point the way to go. Sad ones tell us where NOT to go. Follow your happy and soon you'll feel a bit snappy!

3
Heart to Heart

Place your hand on your heart and say, "I am strong" and feel it ever long!!! So any time you need this INNER STRONG, place your hand on your heart and BOOM — there it is.

4
Together

We are in it together. So help your friends too — teach them to paint a birdhouse, sing a little ditty or smile real pretty. Learning together makes you birds of a feather!

5
Smile

Give a smile away. It's free and spreads glee. It is in your POWER every hour. Enjoy smiling at someone new today, and feel it returned in a BIG way!

6
In Us

In each of us is the INFINITE where we can be grander, more spectacular and amazing than we ever thought possible! Trust you have this INCREDIBLE nature in you and each day you get to let-it-out in a new way. Enjoy discovering your INFINITE NATURE today.

7
The Best

Ordering the best from life and expecting it often returns just that — THE BEST. So enjoy looking for the best in your SELF and OTHERS because soon the best starts looking for you!

8
Courage

Courage is BEING AFRAID but going on anyway, said famous TV anchor Dan Rather. Rather reported the NEWS to the WORLD night after night. It sounds like he had some fright but went ahead ANYWAY with all his might. Do you ever feel afraid, and do it anyway?

9
Believe in YOU

BELIEVE in your ability to DO anything your heart desires. You are a perfect child of God. Look at your FACE in the mirror and proclaim your Greatness! Sing, "I AM GREAT" three times! Oh, yeah.

10
You Are Amazing

You are amazing. Simply amazing! Enjoy living life as the AMAZING you. Look around and see how this world creates AMAZING things for the AMAZING you. You may even say, "I AM AMAZING" and feel it too.

11
Reach For Your Star

Go for it! Reach for your star and you'll go ever far. I so FULLY believe in you reaching your dreams and catching your star. What are you reaching for right now?

12
Focus

Focus on whatever you want to show up! The more you focus on something and believe it will be — the world soon sends it to you for free. What are you focusing upon now?

13
Picture It

Make a picture of your dreams so you see the happy things coming to you! Hang it up somewhere special, and look at it with warm fuzzy feelings. YAY FOR YOU!

14
Never Alone

You are never alone! Every day you are surrounded by love and light in every way. Talk to your angels any time you need a love lift. They instantly help you shift into feeling better and better.

15
Play in Possibility

Play around in the possibilities that surround you. Everything is possible as you play throughout the day. Pigs can fly, dogs can talk and fish can walk. Anything can happen as you play today so enjoy your IMAGINATION in everyway.

16
You can do it!

I believe in YOU and that you can do ANYTHING under the sun. Enjoy making your dreams come true as YOU CAN DO IT TOO. What do you want to do through and through?

17
Everyday

You are loved every minute of every day in every way! I love you. God loves you. Your angels surround you and protect you on your way. There is nothing to fear as you let God steer. Enjoy being surrounded by UNIVERSAL love from above.

18
Dreams Come True

Dorothy in the Wizard of Oz clicked her heels and said, "There's no place like home!" Then she was home. So dreams really do come true. Enjoy dreaming your dream today and letting it come to you.

19
Remember Who You Are

You are a DIVINE being here on earth! Remember this truth as you find your way each and every day. You are here at a special time to bring more light, love, peace and happiness into the rhyme.

20
Hug

Hug someone every day! It can be your teddy bear, doggie woggie or big old self but its important to hug someone every day. It sends the message of love into and out of you in EVERY WAY. Make hugging fun and do it as you feel ONE.

21
Heavenly Day

Every day is a heavenly, heavenly, heavenly day! Celebrate each day as you make it on your way. It feels SO GOOD to celebrate every day and feel its holiness come to play. What is sacred and silly today?

22
Say Its So

Keep your word when you say it's so! It builds your SELF-CONFIDENCE and TRUST as you stand by your word. And people respect you and you are heard. So when you say its so, stand by it as you go.

23
Listen

Each of us has a still small voice within. Learning to listen as it GROWS and GROWS helps us figure out our individual SHOWS. It gives us clues and personal news to light our way each day. Do you want to share what your voice says today?

24
You are DEEPLY loved

You are so deeply, deeply loved in every way. I want you to FEEL so amazingly loved. Loved from your toes to your nose and from your eyes to your thighs there is GREAT love here for you.

25
Magic

The Universe is filled with magic! You are the CREATOR in every way of the magic to be done today. So hum this magical song, "Magic of light and love, shine on me from above!"

26
Earth Angels

Friends are earth angels. They help us over the humps when there are bumps! Each of us needs a hand to hold so we can behold this GREAT LIFE given to us. Thank your EARTH ANGEL today in your own special way.

27
Unfolding Miracles

Everyday is FULL of miracles to unfold your way. Say "Happy Surprises Come to Me" in the morning and see what happens all day. Happy things just find you in all sorts of unexpected ways!

28
Full of Wonder

So many things fill UP this world that are WONDER-FULL to see, hear, do and experience all around. What SPARKS your sense of wonder? Is it a RAINBOW, WATERFALL or SHOOTING STAR? Tell me all about it today.

29
Catch Yourself

Catch yourself mastering something! It may be riding a bike without training wheels, putting together a completely new puzzle or learning a new language. Be positively proud and happy as you master something totally new, cool and completely you!!!

30
Victory

Savor the feeling of victory! Perhaps recently you scored a winning goal on the soccer team, got an A on a test or conquered a fear such as snakes. You did it! This is a message from the universe that recently you WON BIG at something. Smile big at that one!

31
Whatever

Whatever this world sends you, you can solve it! I believe in your abilities to SOLVE anything. You are so STRONG and SMART and CAPABLE of creating solutions wherever you go. Enjoy being part of the solution today.

32
Love

You are loved now, always and forever. My love for you doesn't depend on a single thing. It is constantly flowing like the Niagara Falls, a great big waterfall that is constantly blessing the Earth with watery love.

33
Superhuman

Love gives you superhuman strength! As you love yourself more and more — you can become superhuman strong able to face any day with GREAT LOVE. Enjoy wearing your invisible SUPERHUMAN CAPE of self-love today.

34
Mission

You are on a divine mission! You are sent here from high above to bring GREAT LOVE. So close your eyes, say someone's name and send them the feeling of love — wow, you did it!

35
Never Give Up

Never ever give up! Life has some bumps and bruises, ups and downs, highs and lows but never, ever GIVE UP. Being able to hang on and not give up is a GIFT to yourself that you are STRONG, CAPABLE and WILLING to see life through. Plus there are rewards coming to you.

36
Help from my friends

Sometimes you may need a little help from your friends! Friends are valuable to lift up your spirits or turn a frown upside down. Be sure to make new friends and keep the old. The Girls Scouts say, one is silver and the other is gold.

37
Bright Side

Always in life there is a bright side! But just like dogs need to get potty-trained outside, we people need to get trained too. We need to learn the art of training our mind to look for the happy in every way.   What happy do you see now?

38
Falling Down

Each of us falls down. You might skin your knee, get a bruise or fall off your bike! Even bears fall when they try and stand up too tall. But the important part is not that you fall it's that you PICK YOURSELF UP like a Playful Pup. WOOF, WOOF.

39
Smile

Smiles come from within! The better you feel about YOU the more you can smile through and through. So be happy to be the perfect you.

40
Rainy Days

You wake up and it's raining. You wish there would be sun, but instead you can make indoor fun. Like video games, reading, puzzles, painting or learning about something incredible like the Pyramids in Egypt. Enjoy making the best of whatever weather comes your way today!

41
Loved

YOU ARE SO LOVED. No matter what happens here, there and everywhere — you are loved exactly as you are! I always see you as a rising star.

42
I Can Do It!

Say, "I can do it" and feel the energy booming through you! A "can-do" and "want-to-do" feeling helps you and me. It lets you feel your power that you can REALLY do whatever you set your mind too. What do you want to do now?

43
Full-on

Your moment is here! Don't hold anything back. Play full-on today in every way. Enjoy getting totally involved in something and throwing your whole self into it. It's a great way to play.

44
Be Open to Help

We are all connected! Each of us wants happiness and to avoid pain. Learning to help others be happy and receive help your Self is SPECIAL work. Be open to receiving help today in all sorts of miraculous ways.

45
Truly Are

You are perfect as you TRULY ARE! I see your unique, amazing one-of-a-kind spark — it lights the day in a magical way.

46
Recognition

I see you. I REALLY see you. I SEE all the GREAT things you do and how you interact with others! I feel so happy to be part of your life and really see you as TALENTED, SMART and SILLY. Enjoy letting others see you too!

47
Flow

Going with the flow is the best way to be! It helps you and me. It means cooperation and flexibility. Like a fish floating along with the tides, it smiles as it rides the waves. Can you give me your best fish face?

48
Grace

Each of us is given special talents! Sometimes we do something and fail because it's not our talent. Learning how to fail with grace is a lesson that puts a smile on our face. It means letting things go and getting on with our best show.

49
Sense of Self

Repeat after me: I love me. I love me. I love me. You love me. You love me. You love me. Giving your self these positive words each day creates a herd of love coming your way!

50
The Key

Play is the key! As you play more and more it opens a magical door. The door is one of joy for every girl and boy. So play today, and let everything flow your way.

51
Practice

Practice makes perfect. This is true! When we start something we feel silly and stinky and this is true too. But practice helps so much. It is the magical touch. What are you practicing today?

52
Funny Faces

Show me your funny faces! I heard you can make them in all sorts of places. Give me your best face and it will light up this space.

53
Fully Loaded

You come fully loaded and equipped for this magical world. Everything you need is within you. I am here to help guide your way as you get your Earth legs and play.

54
Pick Yourself Up

Courage is the ability to pick your self up after you feel stinky! Sometimes we all make mistakes, fall down, get sad, lose at a game, fail at test and get picked last for a sport team. But when it happens, let-it-go. Stinky is just part of the human show.

55
Bicycling

Got a bicycle? Love to ride? It feels so free. Like you are riding a horse, wee-wee-wee! You might even have a basket and bells. Or fat tires to go into the dirt. Whatever it may be, enjoy feeling so free!

56
I AM

I AM heaven said Jim Carrey, the actor. "I AM" is a special saying that brings heaven to earth, light to you and creates the world anew. I am happy, I am love, I am joyful like a dove. What "I AM" statement are you now?

57
Together

Playing together helps through all types of weather! Some days feel like sun and others we want to run. A secret to a happy life is staying connected even if it feels like clouds in our heart. Together we can *all* make a new start.

58
Endless

My love for you is endless. It has no beginning and no end. It will always go on and on. I want to take this moment to say "I LOVE YOU, now and always!"

59
Sure-ism

Sure-ism is stronger than optimism, stated Shinn. In other words when you feel ABSOLUTELY positive about something — it often comes to be. So what are you sure about today?

60
Boomerang

Everything comes back to you! Like a boomerang or two... So send happy smiles, silly sounds, playful games, sharing toys and nice words out. Soon you'll see what comes in is joyful like thee. What will you send out today?

61
Heart-to-Heart

Place your hand over your heart to feel calm and safe. All is well. If you ever feel uneasy or scared, you can always put your hand on your heart and remind yourself "ALL IS WELL" and so it is.

62
Song

In the Old Testament of the Bible the word "song" is mentioned more than 225 times! Somehow God, the grand POO BA, loves to sing and dance. What song makes you feel like dancing now?

63
Bear

Bears have great power! They are physically and emotionally strong. These animals hibernate, eat lots of honey, run fast, climb trees, protect baby bears and show no cares. Can you be like a bear today?

64
Miracle

'Live as if EVERYTHING is a miracle," said Einstein. The sun rising, moon setting, birds chirping, clouds passing, flowers blooming, fishes swimming, tadpoles transforming, butterflies flittering — it all seems so miraculous to me. What feels like a miracle to you?

65
All You

You get to make your own life! It's all YOU and our CREATOR. Enjoy making a life as you sing, jump, dance, pee, poop, play and find your way. What will you make anew today?

66
Talent Show

You are so incredibly talented! Maybe you want to make a talent show at home? Mom can sing, dad can play the drums, sister can twirl a baton and you can do your special talent...Have fun with it.

67
Lion

Inside each of us is a strong LION that can do anything!
I see how strong you are right now. Can you show me
your lion's roar? Roar anytime to keep weakness away
from your door.

68
Wonder

Wonder is the natural joy you feel looking at the GREAT
mysteries of life! Like the stars in the sky — how did
they get there? Or caterpillars turning to butterflies —
how does that happen? Enjoy the wonder of learning and
discovering too.

69
Hero

Have a hero! Heroes inspire us. They BRING OUT
THE BEST in us. A secret to a wonderful life is to have
HEROES that speak to your heart. Some heroes of mine
are Buddha and Wonder Woman. Who is your hero today?

70
Golden Link

Every person is a golden link in your chain of good.
Even the person that is stinky is teaching you to be
patient and kind. Stinky people feel stinky themselves.
So instead of PEE-U, say God Bless You.

71
Captain You

You are the captain of your ship. ONLY YOU. Put your hands in front of you like you are steering your very, own boat! Close your eyes, feel the wind, smell the sea air, hear the dolphins and enjoy sailing over smooth waters! Ahoy, mate.

72
Who-Who

Be the owl today! Owls have great big eyes so they can PAY ATTENTION and see in the dark. Look around with OWL eyes today to see everything happening just as its supposed to. Want to show me your owl eyes now?

73
Wish Journal

Make a wish journal that is FULL of your dreams and wishes! Add to it each week. Use stickers, glue, sparkles, colors and paste images from magazines. It will help you dreams come true!!!

74
YES

Say YES three (3) times aloud! Yes, yes and YES!!! See how it feels. A secret to a happy life is to follow that feeling. Where is your YES today?

75
Use Your Voice

Use Your Voice today! Sing a little bit, hum a little tune or say something soft and special. Your voice is uniquely you and I love it through and through.

76
Om

Om away the day today! Om is a sacred healing sound. Can you Om? Would like to Om together?

77
Good Things

Good things come to you. Good things go from you. It is a special feeling to know that you are SAFE in every way! Angels see to it that you are protected today.

78
Celebrate Steps

Every step you take is an important one! And the more you celebrate in life, the more you have to celebrate. So what step shall we be happy about today?

79
Find a Happy Teacher

Happy teachers are like sunshine on a rainy day! They bring us happy teachings and show us the way. Such masters calm our minds and ease our hearts. Can you find a happy teacher today?

80
Life is Fun

Life is supposed to be fun. Play more today and feel the good come your way. A secret to a magical life is to pick work that feels like PLAY!

81
Soup Breath

Hot soup breath is when you take a deep breath in your nose and blow out your mouth like you are cooling soup down! It also has the magical effect of COOLING you down too. Take as many hot soup breaths as you need whenever you need them!

82
Pick Peace

Peace always lives in our heart. It is a calm and happy heart no matter what is going on! If you need to FEEL more peaceful, put your hand over your heart and say, "I am peace" so you feel it through and through — even from me to you!

83
Great People

Really great people make you feel like you too can become great, said Mark Twain. And this is true! Who is GREAT in your life now?

84
Dream Big

You can play as BIG as the dreams you make! Everything is possible. Make a PICTURE of your biggest DREAMS coming true and soon they'll be smiling at you. Hang it up too.

85
Skip to the Colorful You

Colors create our day! Blue helps us rest, yellow brightens us up and green makes us smile. Wear something colorful today that makes you smile in every way!! Forget about matching today and skip to the colorful you!

86
Thanks Banks

Fill your thanks banks! Say "THANK YOU" for all that comes to you such as the sunny day, smelly dog and chance to play. What will you fill your thanks banks with today?

87
Miracles

Miracles come in small and extra large sizes! If you need a miracle for any reason, just ask. Anything is possible if you believe with your whole heart.

88
Stillness Speaks

You can be still anytime to chill. Stillness speaks and may now be speaking to you. A secret to life is learning how to be still. It is in the stillness that secrets reveal themselves to you...

89
Rainbows

Rainbows only come after the rain. Look for the hidden blessing after you feel rain in your heart. Happy surprises often await you after the pain. Learn to look for them!

90
Animal Kind

Every animal has a family just like you! With a spider mommy, daddy, sister or brother too! Be kind to icky-sticky things, slimy bugs, furry friends and old pets as they have feelings and families too.

91
Power

Each of us has great power! We can use it any hour. Like Harry Potter's wand or magic spells that channel our force for good. What are you using your power for this hour?

92
Believing In Yourself

Once you believe in YOU then others can too! So look at yourself, make a list of all the NIFTY things about you and appreciate them. Can you tell me one nifty thing about you now?

93
Only You

You are here to do what ONLY YOU can do. You fill a place that only you can fill. Enjoy being FULLY and completely YOU. WAHOO!

94
Calm Space

Create a calm space. Someplace that makes you feel slow, quiet and nice. It will help if you go there twice. It will bring you peace in every way.

95
Connected Kids

Kids are everywhere! Get connected to a kid somewhere else so you GROW and SHOW each other what being a kid is like here and there. Enjoy this dare.

96
Body Messages

Listen to your body! Does it feel happy and strong? Or sleepy and long? Listen to what it has to say and it will guide you in a new way. Yoga, Tai-Chi or Karate may help in this way today.

97
Positive Energy

Send positive energy out to the world. Do you know what this means? You are like a radio with invisible love waves and you get to send them to anyone, anywhere, any time. Where do you want to send them to now?

98
Bubble Up

Just say "Bubble Up" and a big white bubble will surround you! This will protect you and keep you safe. Say it everyday. That way you'll have your energy and it will fuel your day.

99
Self Trust

Inside of you are the answers. Trust how you feel. Trust what you think. Listen to your inner self whisper, give you nudges, feelings and point the way. Do you trust your feelings as messages? Let's start today.

100
All is Well

In life we don't always feel swell. Remembering that "All is Well" is a divine notion. It is a little saying like a potion. Say "All is Well" to lift up your heart. It reminds us in every moment there is a NEW START.

101
Capable

You are so incredibly capable right now! You can do whatever you set your mind to. What do you want to do, be or learn now? I am sure it will give me a WOW.

102
Stand By Your Word

You are what you say. So be careful and say only what you mean! Your words, like magic spells, have power. Like me saying, "I love you" is really strong and makes your heart happy ever-long.

103
Seeing It

If you can "see" or imagine something it has possibility. Like Alexandar Graham Bell who invented the telephone. He imagined it was possible and then soon it came to be. What are you imagining now?

104
Thank-FULL

Say "THANK YOU" for this day. It is a gift to you in every way. Thank God for things BIG such as the sun, moon and everyone. Thank GOD for things SMALL like a tadpole, fish and flowering wish. The more thanks you GIVE, the more JOY you live.

105
Imperfections

Everyone is perfectly imperfect! That is the joy of being a girl and boy. Earth is where we come to polish ourselves. It is our spirit that is without flaw. So enjoy openly growing and showing your joyful imperfect self.

106
The Journey

Life is really a journey. A path. A way that is always teaching us to grow, learn and expand. Let go of pain. Learn to live with more love. What are you learning on your path today?

107
Life Loves Me

"Life loves me," stated Louise Hay. Those are powerful words to lift you up. Repeat them now and anytime!

108
Connected

What you say sends signals and feelings to others. So how can you make a happier world today? Maybe a smile, dance or song...

109
Think You Can

If you think you can, you can. If you think you can't, you are right explained Henry Ford. A secret to success in life is BELIEVING you can do it. I certainly believe you can!

110
Courage

Courage is when you feel a little shaky and do something anyway! Like when you first took off the training wheels on your bike. It was scary. But soon you were riding smoothly without any help. Where do you need courage to show-up today?

111
Confidence

Confidence means to believe in your Self! Like when you jumped off the diving board for the first time, you believed you could do it. And you did. Enjoy believing in yourself more and more. It's a secret to feeling happy.

112
See Your Skills

I see how skilled you are right now! It's amazing to see your talents come out to play, and brighten my day. You just have such a knack for _____.

113
Trust

Trust is when you believe someone! Like when my sister promised she wouldn't look at my secret journal. And she didn't. I trust her now to stay out of my things. It feels REALLY good to trust.

114
Listen to Your Self

Learning to LISTEN to your SELF is trust. Inside each of us are all the answers. I pay attention to HOW I FEEL to guide my way. I look to follow my GOOD FEELINGS everyday.

115
Skills

Turning strengths to skills can be really, really fun! Like my drawing ability I use to make maps and books. I feel really, really skilled at it now. What makes you feel super-duper skilled?

116
Magic Wands

Words are like magic wands! They shape your world. What you say often happens. So say something smart and fun. Like, "I love everyone!"

117
Miracles

Miracles are life's unexplainable events that make things magically better but no one can explain WHY. Like when really, really sick people have amazing recoveries or when things are way lost and become found like Wilbur the cat. Meow. Meow. Do you believe in miracles too?

118
Connection

Fieldtrips are great ways to CONNECT with other kids and people as you learn new things. My class took a field trip to see the LIBERTY BELL in 8th grade. What does your class do?

119
Good is On the Way

So among all the things you see today realize that there is some good coming your way. Even if someone is grumpy or bumpy! Good is always looking for you, poo poo pa do.

120
Strong

You are strong inside. There's no need to hide. You can enjoy living from your strong place as you go through this time and space. Live Strong.

121
Better

Every day gets a little bit better! Ever notice that?
Sometimes it's a little step better and other times it's a
big better. What has gotten better for you lately?

122
Believe

I believe fully in YOU. You can do, be or have ANYTHING
in the whole wide world and I'll cheer you on day-by-day.
So let's start now and cheer away! YAY, Yay, Yay!

Section II
Educating

It is very important to generate a good attitude, a good heart, as much as possible. From this, happiness both in the short and long term for both yourself and others will come.

His Holiness the Dalai Lama

Education

literally means "to bring up" or "to bring out" and "to lead" as derived from Latin.

Educating children

is a process of guiding them to bring out their best selves – with skill and awareness.

Educating a child's heart and mind is crucial. I believe it is the difference between a kinder, calmer and more generous child versus the opposite. Like the acorn that holds the latent potential of the oak tree within it, every child holds his or her potential. And it is in educating a child's mind as well as heart that enables those potentials to come to life and last.

So what type of education was I missing as a child? The laws of cause and effect (i.e. karma), the truth of suffering (i.e. attachment), the interconnected nature of humanity, the nature of emotions (i.e. they change), antidotes for common negative emotions (i.e. patience for anger) and the root of persistent positive emotions (i.e. thinking of others). YES – these would have helped tremendously!

Each sounds like a complex topic. And it is. The reality is that such multi-layered topics can be explained in simple words to children. Suzanne, age 7, learned that when she helps her elderly neighbor, she feels great. Margie, her mother, reinforced this concept by picking the saying, "Helping others also brings happy feelings to you" and Suzanne is beginning to grasp it.

Such educating sayings will plant the seeds of *a skillful worldview* – one that benefits him or herself as well as others.

Educating Kids: The 5 Key Areas

Standard schooling systems often overlook cultivating key aspects that propel a child's best life such as their emotional health, ethics, compassion and wisdom. It is this type of education focused upon in this section via the five key areas below.

Character Development	It is the development of ethics and integrity in each child. Universal concepts are suggested such as honesty, respect, truth, self-discipline, kindness and equanimity.
Emotional Awareness	It is the development of emotional health in each child. This includes the ability to understand the nature of emotions, how to regulate them, provide coping skills and suggest emotions as indicators. The seeds of peace and happiness are planted as well.
Social Learning	It is the development of social skills that benefit self and others. This includes valuing teamwork, differences and beginning to understand that we are all connected.

Service Learning	It is the development of a helping attitude and experience in life. Universal concepts such as gratitude, generosity, compassion and love are explored.
Universal Truths	It is the development of basic insight into universally accepted truths. Such concepts include peace education, roots of happiness and karma (law of cause and effect).

Impacting how a child begins crafting his or her worldview happens everyday. It is usually the little things that spur big realizations. Each aspect above applies to every child. You may want to further tweak some of the sayings to fit your particular lifestyle, culture or religious affiliation.

Savor making the sayings your own. Fill them with sincerity and enthusiasm – your child will feel it through and through!

Tips

- **E**mpty your mind of any outstanding clutter right now.

- **G**et into a positive state of mind.

- **F**ocus on *playfully* and *purposefully* EXPANDING your child's understanding.

- **P**ick a saying that really speaks to you.

- **S**peak to your child with 100% enthusiasm, sincerity and authority.

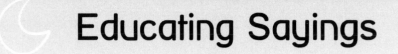

123
Patch

Each of us is like a patch. Together we make a beautiful quilt joining all our different patches of color, cultures and creations. It is in celebrating such uniqueness and differences that we discover our own creative genius.

124
Stick-to-it-ness

Each of us wants to create something! It takes stick-to-it-ness to complete a creation. It is fun to begin something (like painting a birdhouse!) but it requires effort and focus to finish. Make the effort today to see something to completion — it will feel great.

125
The Right Thang

Doing the right thing is ALWAYS the right thing. You see whatever you do — it returns back to you. So if you are nice it will come back twice. If you are grumpy it will come back and feel bumpy. Always remember the right thang is just the right thang!

126
Kindness

Be kind, for everyone you meet is fighting a harder battle, stated Plato. I believe this to be true. You never see what is going on inside. Adults often hide their troubles until they bubbles. So be kind since it is the cure for sure!

127
Sharing is Caring

The more you share — the more you show you care! It is hard for little ones to know how to share. Such babes think me, me and me. You are here to show that it's all for WE not just ME. So share away today.

128
Love

Get lost in something you love! Be it climbing a tree or painting silly.   It's the feeling of flow that creates an imaginative show. All is well as you unfold and bring forth your brilliance so bold.

129
Happy Wishes

Everyone is the same. We all want happiness and to avoid pain. This truth connects every person. No matter what is occurring in life — look past the surface and see every person wants to feel happy. Even the grumpy teacher!

130
Harmony

It's AMAZING that so many different people live together in mostly harmony! Harmony is the ability to be the PERFECT YOU and get along with all the DIFFERENT other people smoothly. Like if a hippo, turkey, monkey and elephant were loving friends to the ends.

131
No Better

There is no better. Each of us is UNIQUE and SPECIAL.
No one is better than anyone else. Every person has gifts
that are being birthed within them EVERY MINUTE.
Respect the blossoming of everyone's gifts equally.

132
Happy

Helping others brings happy feelings to you! So look
for ways to give a helping hand, give a smile away or do
good in some completely original way. Any ideas?

133
The Creativity Cure

Being creative helps exit stinky feelings. So anytime
you feel low — go play in the sand, paint, sing, dance
or move around to exit negative feelings. You are the
active captain of your ship. Exit the stinky crew so you
feel anew.

134
Colors

Colors are feelings too! Yellow is happy. Red is mad.
Green is grateful. Pink is love. Blue is soft. Grey is sad.
Purple is quiet. Orange is play. White is pure light. So
enjoy feeling these colors throughout the day! What
color are you now?

135
Grey Day

If you have a grey day you can change it in every way!
Use your breath to let the grey go. Soon you'll feel a
better show. Exit the sticky and icky feelings from you.
Let them go, go, go! (Breathe them out)

136
Words

Words are powerful. Each one is infused with the
strength of the sun! Say only the ones that you mean as
they create what is seen. If you want to do something
say YES and if not, say NO. Be clear as you use your
words to steer.

137
Changes

Everything you see changes! Summer goes to Fall.
Little becomes tall. Skinny gets wide. Sun comes out
then clouds make it hide. Learning to let things come
and go is the natural flow. What is coming, and going
for you now?

138
Till the End of Time

Close your eyes. Feel your breath coming and going. It
makes its way to the center of you. It finds the space
in you that touches eternity. That connects you to
something greater beyond time and space...

139
Ripple Effect

Life has a ripple effect! Like skipping a rock on the waters edge. You throw it and it bounces on the top of the sea — wee, wee, wee. What you do and say sends messages out in the day. So smile now and you'll show others how.

140
Aware

Be aware of your stare. Use your eyes to shine light. Others are feeling the darkness of night. Your eyes show how joyful and kind is your mind. So smile away and send love through your eyes all day!

141
Rest

Let your mind rest. Clear it out. Sometimes like spring-cleaning in a house, you need to get rid of clutter and junk. So close your eyes and let your mind be still. It is the fuel to refill.

142
Tadpoles

Ever see a tadpole? It is amazing! They are little baby frogs that don't look anything like frogs. They come out of an egg and swim in the water. One day they grow legs and walk out of the water. Their transformation is INCREDIBLE just like the INCREDIBLE YOU.

143
Bully Kindness

Be kind to bullies. They are the hardest to love but need it the most. They don't feel very good inside so they hide behind meanness. Try to see the truth of their pain. Wish them well as you go on to feel swell.

144
Mother Earth

Mother Earth is sharing her energy with thee. Be kind in return. Recycle, pick up trash and take care of her paths. Be loving to her trees, seas, skies and animals ever wise. Say thanks on your way and she'll help you have a good day!

145
Money Matters

Money is energy. It is given to you for your creativity. It is helpful for safety and security. Use it in ways that give to you and others in countless ways. Think of one way to help another with money today.

146
Go Slow

Ever hear of the turtle and the hare? It was the turtle that won the race. The rabbit or hare ran so fast she didn't even last. The turtle went slow and won the whole show. Take time and go slow today — each step needs to be thoughtful in every way.

147
Emotions

Allow emotions to come and go. They all have their own flow. They are not lasting. Emotions are like clouds floating by. They say HI. But soon enough the real stuff inside — natural happy — shines out like an inner sun smiling at everyone!

148
Inner Guide

Connect to your wise guide inside. It tells you when to eat, sleep and hide. Trust your self in every way. You'll never go astray.

149
Heart Songs

Find what makes your heart sing! And follow it with all your might. It will keep brightening your light. So smile today and look for what makes your heart sing in every way.

150
Patience

Patients are not just for doctors! It is the ability to rest in knowing all is well, others can go first, and you can happily wait your turn. There is no RUSH in life. All the best things are coming to you so just be happy and let them SHOW UP right on time...

151
Cycles

Everything goes away. Even today. It is the cycle of life.
Sun rises and sets. Moon rises and sets. Ocean tide
comes into shore and goes out for more. Allowing the
natural circle of life to flow will help you as you go.

152
This Too Will Pass

Sometimes we stub our toe and get upset with this
whole human show. It makes us mad and not even an
ounce glad. All feels wrong. The truth is this too will
pass. Just like a little gas!

153
Hoops

Shooting hoops is such a fun sport! In the moment that
you are shooting you cannot be anywhere else. You
must be 100% focused upon getting the ball into the net.
It is this type of concentration that helps you succeed in
life. Enjoy shooting hoops soon or doing something with
this level of FOCUS.

154
Water

Water washes away dirt. It doesn't hurt. Water grows
our flowers and makes happy rain showers. Explore
water today. It may be washing your hands, running in
a sprinkler or going into water like a bath. ENJOY the
element of WATER today!

155
Motion

Everything is in motion. You say a kind word and it moves out of you! You put something in play as you speak each day. So send out the nice and it will return to you twice.

156
Free

You are born to be free! You are here with me just temporarily. I help you grow and you'll get on with your own show. You get to pick what to do, have or be so that you smile as you feel free ~ wee, wee.

157
Born

Each of us is born in our birthday suit! We all came here looking very cute. It's like our costume in this play. Wear it proudly each and everyday. Clean it up and wash it down. Make it twinkle like a star so it can take you REALLY far.

158
Best

Parents are doing their best! Sometimes they need to rest. Days are long and sometimes they sing a ho-hum song. So smile their way and help them today.

159
Truth

Speak your truth. State what you know and it will show. You will light the way for others today. Some feel fear as the truth comes near. Stand strong and show the truth ever long.

160
Gentle Giants

Manatees are gentle giants. Learn about them. They eat grass and plants. They move slowly and are curious. Many of them live in Florida, West Africa and near the Amazon Basin. Learn about these kind characters today.

161
Express Yourself

A secret to a happy life is to EXPRESS YOURSELF. Inside of you is a BRILLIANCE that is being called out. It is your creative spark. So enjoy expressing your UNIQUE self today and feel happy in every way!

162
Effort

Dreams come true with effort! So many people wish upon a lucky star but forget to work. It takes EFFORT and FAITH to make your dreams come true. Effort means focused trying and FAITH means a belief that YOU CAN DO IT.

163
Working Together

It's really great to work together! Say for example, Pamela the pig was building a house. She needs Jolly the giraffe to put the roof on and Lucy the lion to hold the walls together. Only with teamwork can Pamela get her pig-house. Oink, oink!

164
Hunch

Hunches are the hounds of heaven, stated Shinn. Our instincts inform us. They give us guidance. Such hunches when followed, will not lead you astray. In other words trust your Self — your hunches will show you the way.

165
Energetic Boundaries

You are so incredibly sensitive and sometimes you "pick up" other peoples energy! I have a cure for you. You can say "through me and not to me" so that other energy does not get stuck on you. You want only your energy so you can BE FULLY YOU.

166
Healing Touch

Hands heal so much just through touch. You can hug, shake or hold the healing I am told. Lay your hands on someone's heart and feel the light as you start. You can send love through your fingers from above.

167
Puzzle

Each of us is a puzzle piece. The puzzle is the Planet Earth. Each of us fits with each other interconnected in this puzzle. It's really AMAZING as we work together how much we can positively change our world!!!! What part of the puzzle are you today?

168
Live

Eating food that was live is MOST healthy! This means vegetables, fruits and fish. Look for things to eat that make you feel great — like strawberries, yogurt, bananas and blueberries!

169
Bless

Bless your food. Use whatever words come from your heart. My friend used to say "Rub a Dub-Dub, Thanks for the Grub, Yeah God" and it made him smile and feel grateful. Say whatever sings to your heart.

170
Adore

As you adore something — you allow more! So adore your day and be grateful in every way. Smile at the surprises. Be thankful for the bumps. Everything gets you over the humps.

171
Gentleness Too

Being gentle is good for you. It means softly petting your pup and smiling wide up. It means slowly walking and quietly talking. It's building inner power for every hour. Let gentleness guide your way and feel peace today.

172
Forgive

Growing is fast! Every day you move past your last. Sometimes as we grow there is pain that comes into the show. Kids kick, shout and scream about. It's good to forgive such kids as they are just learning how to happily live.

173
Be True

Sometimes kids pressure you to be part of the choosen few! I prefer you just BE YOU. Fitting in is overrated. Being the beautiful unique you is how you'll grow happy through and through.

174
Thoughts

Thoughts are real. As you think something it comes to be! The more you think it — the more it has possibility. Use your mind to create positive things and feel them come with wings.

175
Hippo

Hungry, hungry hippo was a game! It had a funny name. It was a playful way to make hippos eat and it was a real treat. Play a game today and feel good in every way.

176
Source

Every child is a PERFECT child of God. You don't need to change in ANY way just enjoy your earthly stay. If you need help — just learn to yelp! Angels above will shower you with love.

177
Follow the Smiles

Smiles lead the way. They show YOUR best day! Look for the things that make you SMILE and keep DOING THEM across the mile. Smiles put happy in your heart in every way. What makes you smile today?

178
Years

Many people have years. Sometimes these have fears. Let them be old. Be nice to them and not cold. It's called respect. It doesn't hurt so what the hect.

179
Foster Joy

Bring more happy today! Let the pain go. Send it away with crayons, singing or dancing in a new way. Joy wants to be found. It comes in all sorts of sound. Have fun making joy — boy, oh, boy.

180
Beauty

Let beauty in. It will inspire you and help you win! What is beauty to you? Is it climbing a tree? Or hearing a flute played with glee? Could it be an ice cream cone? Or maybe your dog bone? Beauty makes your HEART SOAR and opens a JOYFUL DOOR.

181
Truth

Truth wakes you up. It cuts through the crap and makes lies take a nap. It sets you free. And it gives you the fuel of honesty. It enables you to be FULLY happy. So be alive and let truth jive!

182
Snowflake

Every snowflake is special. It is UNIQUE and DIFFERENT than every other. Just like you — unique and special too! So perhaps you want to make a snowflake out of paper, list special things about you and hang to feel super good too.

183
Seeing the Best

Others have bumps, bruises and moles on the outside. Often their best qualities hide inside. Like a platypus that looks funny with a silly nose. But when you get to know one he is really sweet, kind and a treat. So have fun looking for the inner platypus in everyone!

184
Check Your Area

Check your area! Keep it clean. Comb your hair. Smile and be seen. Others see the outside of you — so make it clean and pristine. Show your best face and dress up any space.

185
Dream

Imagine the day is the dream. And the night is real. What happens in your dreams? Is it what it seems? Do they have something to say? Or are they silly in every way? I want you to see the day as divine, special and a real goldmine.

186
Coming and Going

Shirts come and go! My favorite shirt got spots of paint — so I had to let it go. Soon I got another that was from my mother. I loved it even more. But I learned to let things in and let things go. It makes for an easier life and smoother flow.

187
Zzzzzz's

Closing your eyes at night and sleeping tight is so cool.
It helps you refuel. You need the rest so you can be your
BEST. SO enjoy snuggling up tonight and waking up
feeling every BRIGHT.

188
Flow

Let your feelings flow. Let them in and let them go. See
them pass. Like clouds up in the sky. They just float by.
Behind them all is sunny smiles to help you across the
miles.

189
Self-discipline

Feelings are so strong. We want it right away — we
can't wait long! Instant getting doesn't help much.
Learning to be happy wherever you are with whatever
you have is the real key. It is your hidden glee.

190
Fairies

Fairies are real. You can call on them to heal. They
come from nature with special gifts. Each of them helps
your heart lift. So draw a fairy, and let the magic in!

191
Positive & Strong

Be positive and strong with your Self. Say "ALL IS WELL" as you go about your day focusing on school and play. It's really swell to be HAPPY and RESPONSIBLE in all you do for me, and you.

192
Great Minds

Great minds discuss ideas; average mind discuss events; small minds discuss people, stated Eleanor Roosevelt. So First Lady Roosevelt's message is not to talk about other kids, and teachers BUT to use your GREAT MIND to have great ideas like how to bring more peace to the planet. Whaddya say?

193
Life

The nature of life is always changing! Things are coming and going. Like the leaves on a tree grow and then fall. Snow comes and then goes. Sun shines and then sets. A secret to life is being happy about the changes that occur in and around us. What is changing for you now?

194
Powers

Use your powers for great things! Do you know where your powers are now? They are on your TONGUE, in your MIND, in your HEART and on your FEET. It is what you SAY, THINK, DO, FEEL and SEE that shape your everyday.

195
Nothing

Nothing comes from nothing. Julie Andrews sang that in The Sound of Music! It means that everything has a cause. All things in life are linked. So plant happy sounds, and see what comes around.

196
More

There is always more to do! So enjoy the process as you go through. Never think you are done. There's always more fun. Classes to take, projects to do, people to meet and places to go too! Enjoy becoming more each and every day.

197
Purple

Be your purple self. Whatever color of the crayon you feel — just be happy to be it!!!! It feels good to be like the other colors and kids but your UNIQUENESS is where your talents live.

198
Pinocchio

Pinocchio was a puppet that told a lie! And in this magical story his nose grew really long from his lie. Then everyone knew his words weren't true. Do you know this story? It is true that people know if you lie — they can feel it in their hearts.

199
Magic

I have always believed in magic, stated Jim Carrey. He's a great actor! The magic he uses is affirmations. He told himself, "I AM a successful actor" so many times that it happened in real life. WOWEEE. What do you magically want to create now?

200
Kid Connection

Some kids live on mountaintops while others live in the middle of the desert. Each has a special gift that when joined together gives the whole planet a lift. Get connected with a kid somewhere else to LEARN, GROW and SHOW your connection.

201
Happy-ness

Happiness grows when you help others. The more you think of SOMEONE else the happier you feel. Soon you realize your little problems go away. And more happy feelings come to stay.

202
Chameleon

Like a chameleon can change colors, you can adapt to any situation! You are flexible and colorful. It is a great quality to be able to go with the flow. You can fit in and become part of your environment easily and effortlessly. Smile today as you flow in every way.

203
Multiplying Kindness

Every act of kindness is multiplied. Give something away today. Your kind word, thank you note or gift helps lift a heart ~ then THAT person smiles more to someone else, spreading your KINDNESS everywhere.

204
Unanswered Prayers

Thank God for unanswered prayers! Sometimes we pray for things that aren't the best for us. We just don't know at the time. God listens to all prayers. He answers them too. Sometimes the answer is nothing so you can be the BEST YOU.

205
Tears

Tears are the words that the heart cannot say. It is true. Let your tears flow as your emotions go. Show the world you cry and don't apologize why. Tears show you are strong and feel deep and long.

206
Pledge

Pledge to make a happy mind. When mad, sad or scared come up — show them the door. Say goodbye. Let them go. Feel them out. Even scream or shout them through. It will help you feel anew.

207
Space

Make your own special space! It can feel like a
SPACESHIP or TREEHOUSE but whatever it is make it
feel cool to you. You need a spot to recharge your battery
and not get too hot. It will be a magical place that will
be a healing space JUST FOR YOU.

208
Friend

Make friends with your self. Be KIND to you. Take care
of your body. Feed it healthy foods. Enjoy cleaning it.
And say nice things to it. All of it counts. The nicer you
are to YOU, the more you can do.

209
Anything

Anything is possible! Like the movie Enchanted - life
seems to never end the way we think it will. Often it is
even better. Be open to the SURPRISES life brings you.
And know no matter what, you will BE WELL through
and through.

210
Furry Friend

Make a furry friend till the end. It may be a PUPPY or
KITTEN you know. Or perhaps it is a stuffed PENGUIN
that shares time with you. Whatever it is, talk to it,
smile with it, pet it nice and realize it loves you twice.

211
Truth

The Buddha says you cannot hide three things. Do you know what they are? He said it is the MOON, SUN and TRUTH. The truth always comes out so it is BEST to tell the truth first thing.

212
Your Best

Do your best then let it all go! Your best efforts always show. Whatever happens — you know you put your best FOOT forward. That is the mark of a winner!

213
Steps

Life is full of stepping-stones. Like you crossing a river. You got from one rock to the next — each one taking you further across the waters! Enjoy each step.

214
Here

Here is the only TIME that exists. Yesterday is gone, tomorrow hasn't happened so HERE is all there is now. ENJOY being HERE now.

215
Butterfly

Butterflies remind us that we change. Every day is a new and important discovery along the way. Our lives, bodies, minds and feelings change. Allow for the joyful process of change in your life — whatever that might be!

216
Unexpected

Sometimes life gives us the unexpected! Shiva the pug
puppy was tossed into the river. He never swam before.
But he just KNEW how to swim. Remember you know
so much more than you think you do! And TRUST you
can swim through it too.

217
Na-na

It feels great to get NA-NA. That is naked without
clothes in the bath or running around the house.
Sometimes life and clothes are too much. Enjoy being
a kid and running around with EVERYTHING hanging
out, even your cutie batootie.

218
Kindness

Kindness is being nice. Nice is a beautiful quality of
a person. The nicer you are, the nicer you feel and the
nicer surrounds you like a protective seal.

219
Tree Trunks

Climbing a tree can give you a WHOLE new perspective
on life. You are up in the air feeling high and free. It
helps you feel happy and glee. Experience being with a
TREE today in a magical way!

220
Peace

Peace is calmness. It is not wanting anything. It is stillness. It is joy. It is feeling a happy heart and being full of calm love. What makes you feel most at peace?

221
On

There is never nothing going on. Keep your eyes open to life! Pay attention to everything going on. The more your eyes and mind are open — the more you get to SEE and BE.

222
Silly

Being silly is serious business! The more you laugh — the more happy things comes to find you. So look for the LAUGHS in whatever situation you are in right now and find something silly. It's good for YOU and EVERYONE too.

223
Joy

Feeling lots of happy inside is Joy. Joy is considered IMMEASURABLE — it can be so big, spread so far and make you shine like a star. Follow your joy.

224
Look Within

Looking within will give you answers. Always "SEE" how your heart feels and use your feelings as a guide. Follow your happy heart feelings to make a JOYFUL day.

225
THANK YOU

"Thank you" are two very important words! It not only shows an ATTITUDE of GRATITUDE but grows a happy and great-full heart. Thank away today.

226
Woodpecker

Woodpeckers awaken you to opportunities. When opportunity knocks, answer the door, is a well-worn saying. What opportunities are knocking at your door? And have you seen a woodpecker lately?

227
Helping Hands

Give someone a helping hand today! You might hold a door open, help someone with a heavy bag or set the dinner table. Let your helping hands grow a happy heart for yourself.

228
Less is More

Often less words go farther. So avoid being a CHATTERBOX about nothing. Pick your words carefully and say more with less. Like "I love you" and "Thank You" and "I am sorry" are all powerful words.

229
Doors

Holding open doors helps everyone! It is kindness in action. It seems small but it is these small acts that grow kindness tall.

230
Teamwork

Being part of a whole team is more than the sum of each member. Acting as a team with common goals has the power to create magic! Ever watch an Olympic team?

231
Pitching In

Pitching in helps each of us win! A few hands are better than one. By helping someone or someplace out — it shows your ability to be part of a solution. Look for ways to pitch in!

232
Letting Go

Pee out your problems. Let them go, go, go! Poop
out what you no longer need. Bye, bye, bye. Letting
everything come into you and go out is VERY
IMPORTANT. So enjoy taking the best from life and
letting go of the rest!

233
Ups and Downs

Life feels like a ROLLERCOASTER with high ups and low
downs. Don't be fooled though — the feelings of scared,
mad, glad and sad pass. Be brave as you show the low
feelings the door and ask for the happy ones to come
MORE and MORE.

234
Playful

Puppies are playful. You see their tails WAG and WHOLE
bodies wiggle & giggle. It is this PLAYFUL way that
brings smiles today. Enjoy wagging your invisible tail
today as you play, play and PLAY.

235
Create

We are creators! That is why we are here. Use your
talents and orginality as you create away. What might
you want to create today?

236
Be the Bunny

Put the best in your body! It makes all the difference in the world. Put green vegetables, oranges and lots of healthy things in so you can hop around like a little BUNNY. Be the bunny. And act very funny!

237
Inner and Outer

Your INNER world of thoughts and feelings creates your OUTER WORLD. Look at Barack Obama. He THOUGHT and FELT like he could be President. And now he is President. What do you think on the inside?

238
Attraction

You attract what you are, stated Wayne Dyer. So BE a person of kindness, love, playfulness and joy and you'll see more of THAT in your life.

239
Peace

The way of peace is the way of truth, stated Ghandi. A sense of peace always exists when someone is COURAGEOUSLY speaking their truth. Be true to yourself today and feel the peace in every way.

240
Action

Camera, lights, ACTION! This is what Film Directors say in Hollywood. W. Clement Stone was also a big believer in moving your dreams into action. What dream of yours do you want to make happen now?

241
Living

You can make a life by doing what you most enjoy!!! What do you most enjoy lately?

242
Truth

When in doubt, tell the truth, said Mark Twain. The truth may be uncomfortable but it does set you free. It frees up your much needed energy so you can be happily and fully you.

243
Appreciate

Being thankful and feeling grateful is APPRECIATION. And the more you appreciate others and thank them — the more great people just magically show up. Who are you thankful for today?

Section III
Inspiring

Imagination is the preview of life's coming attractions.

Albert Einstein

Inspiration

literally means "to blow" or
"to breathe" life or spirit into...
something or someone.

Inspiring children

is a process of connecting them to
something greater that breathes life
into their dreams.

Children live in a world of creativity, imagination and inspiration. Keeping kids connected to this sphere as well as cultivating this creative connection is the focus of this section. Even more specifically, inspiring sayings encourage your child to connect with his or her:

◆ Imagination

◆ Creativity

◆ Intuition

◆ Spirit

◆ Sense of Beauty (Art, Music, Nature)

Sections one and two were about giving your child roots. This section is about giving your child wings. Like Muhammad Ali explains, anyone who has no imagination has no wings. So with a rooted positive self-concept and worldview, your child is free — free to explore, create, imagine, play, dream and become more.

Inspiration: A Creative Connection

Inspiration is the feeling of being connected to something greater. It is Mulder's search for the truth, His Holiness the Dalai Lama's commitment to free sentient beings from suffering, it is Oprah's commitment to improve education for girls in Africa and it is James Taylor's ability to channel great songs. Getting and staying inspired is a very personal experience.

Children are often naturally inspired by life, and their everyday new experiences. It *becomes even more powerful* when the awakened adults around them consciously help them connect with their:

Imagination
To ponder and see something before it is actually in physical form. It is the mark of original thinkers, innovators and problem solvers.

Intuition
A connection to one's inner wisdom (i.e. hearing, feeling and sensing). Self-trust is required.

Spirit
A connection to non-physical energy (i.e. dreams, prayers, thoughts, feelings).

Sense of Beauty
A quality of something that is lovely to the senses of the mind, body and spirit. Beauty often inspires creativity (i.e. nature, art, music).

Creativity
The tapping of one's own imagination in producing something completely new (i.e. poetry, painting, mathematical formula, house decorating etc...).

Nurturing a child's imaginative, creative and intuitive abilities is essential to his or her unique expression. Along with this encouragement children, like everyone, deeply wish to connect to something greater that further inspires their talents to come to life. Such inspiring connections may involve Beauty, Art, Music, Words, Nature and Spirit.

Tips

- **L**et-go of your past and future. Be completely here now.

- **R**elax into feeling ALL IS WELL and recall what has inspired you.

- **F**ocus on encouraging your child's natural connection to what inspires him or her.

- **S**elect a saying that feels just right for this moment.

- **G**ive your child the gift of your UNDIVIDED attention.

244
Swings

Swings remind us to be happy! You feel so free with the wind in your hair and not one single care. It feels like great joy. Boy, oh boy. Shall we make a date to see a swing soon?

245
Frogs Leap

Everyday there is a frog that leaps really far! Ever feel like a frog? Can you move like one too? The feeling of a frog is a joyful way to go about your day happily hopping from one lily pad to another to play.

246
Beauty

Ever see something unbelievably beautiful? Like a great sunset that is pink, purple, blue, yellow and gold. Or fireworks way up in the sky that are magical I am told. Look for the beauty today in everyway.

247
Inspiration Loop

Everyday is full of magic in all sorts of ways. The more you play, let it in and hop about your day — the feel-good feelings come and go to inspire your best show. What magic did you see today?

248
Greatness

Ever feel like you are in the presence of greatness? Like when you see an AMAZING artist, ballet dancer, or baseball player perform right before your very eyes. That amazement is the feeling of being in front of greatness!

249
Adventure

Have an adventure or two. WAHOO. It gives us the delight of feeling so pure and light. Making life an adventure creates a happy-go-lucky feeling of fun for everyone. What adventure is new for you?

250
Moving Right Along

Moving right along foot loose and fancy free, I am ready for the big-time but is it ready for me, said Kermit the Frog. Do you know Kermit? He likes to sing and dance. Do you have dancing feet?

251
Lightening Bugs

Lightening bugs light up the whole night. They are so funky and spunky! Their tails get really bright and send off some light. Can you wiggle your tail? Does it make life feel a little bright?

252
Mirrors

Ever have someone look at you and make you feel
TERRIFIC TOO! Its like they can see your greatness
and send it back to you. I look at you now, and feel a
great sense of WOW. Enjoy wowing everyone today.

253
Silly Opposites

Some say opposites attract. Like tall and short, skinny
and wide, silly and serious! Like if Harry the Hippo
married Jilly the Giraffee or Frank the Frog married
Betty the Butterfly. What silly opposites are speaking
to you?

254
Upside Down

Look at something upside down! If it's right side up,
turn it upside down. It changes everything so you can
see life anew. If you ever get stuck use this tool through
and through.

255
New

Try something new today! It may be small or BIG in a
new way. Try to sing if you usually dance or roll in the
mud if you usually prance. Enjoy doing something new
as that is how good things come JUST TO YOU.

256
Pig for a Day

Can you pretend to be a pig for a day? It would help you in every way. You can OINK, OINK and OINK. Or roll in the mud. Or shake your curly tail as you get the mail. Let's play for a bit today.

257
Look Up

Look up to someone in your life. It may be a teacher who treats you nice! Or a friend that calls you twice. Find someone that makes your heart happy and look up to him or her for happy advice.

258
Touch

Use your hands to touch the world and create anew. Put your hands in paint or touch the glue. Maybe even plant a flower, move a worm or wave hello this hour. Get in touch with your feeling of touch and it will make you happy so much.

259
Courage

Every act of courage is rewarded a thousand times over. It takes courage to try something new! What is it that you are trying to do?

260
Talk Dog?

Do you talk dog? Animals communicate with us all the time. Birds chirp to invite friends over to their birdhouse! Cats purr because they love being scratched. And dogs wag their tails when they are happy! So can you talk dog, cat or bird?

261
Unseen

So much in life is unseen. It's as if there is a big magical dream. So let me remind you that all that you see is not all that there is… do you agree?

262
Be True

Be true to you. I always love being true to me. It helps me be happy. So as you go about your day and play — remember to be true to you and do what it is happy to you.

263
Sounds Spark Me

Listen for sounds that make you happy! Like birds chirping, pretty music on the stereo and friends that say hello. Hearing the happy sounds that surround your day is a secret to finding your happy way.

264
Make Some Noise

Clap some pots and pans together! Or use a drum, or find a kazoo to make you feel WAHOO. Making noise is good for you, and it lets out all the icky feelings and stuck emotions that make you want to shout. Go make some noise!

265
Skunk

Skunks smell stinky! Like a kid that never washes his winky. But I think you smell good as all kids should. So tell me about your favorite smells?

266
Elephant Ears

Put on your elephant ears! They help you listen to all the things going on that are LOUD and soft. So enjoy listening with elephant ears all day as you find your soft way.

267
Imaginary Friends

Everyone has imaginary friends! They help us to no ends. Like angels, fairies and leprechauns they show us the way when we go astray. So ask away and they'll help you today.

268
Flow

Feeling in the flow is the only way to go! Life feels busy sometimes but that isn't the best show. Take each day at a time, and feel the beauty of the natural flow...Nice and slow, there you go!

269
Everyday Beauty

Can you see everyday beauty? Like the yellow dandelions against the green grass. Or sun so bright it sends happy light. Or the bird nests up high keeping them safe in the sky. Look for beauty today in every way.

270
Find Your Thing

What is your thing? The thing that you really, really want to learn about today — you are kind of obsessed about it in a good way.

271
Happy Inside

Let yourself be happy inside. Pursue a playful path that makes you feel light, and happy no matter what's happening at home or school. What makes you happy right now?

272
Be a Good One

Abraham Lincoln was one of the best Presidents of the United States. He said, "Whatever you are — be a good one." I see so much good in you. What do you want to be "a good one" at today?

273
When I Do Good, I Feel Good

Lincoln said, "When I do good, I feel good. When I do bad, I feel bad." It's a universal law that whatever you do, returns to you. How do you feel right now?

274
Space

Pigs in Space was a super great Muppet Movie Skit! What do you imagine in space today? Do you want your very own spaceship? Or space suit so you can move through the galaxies boldly and go where no one has gone before...

275
Under the Sea

Under the sea you might find me! I am a starfish who swims and floats as all the boats go by and by. What might you want to see that lives near me?

276
Dolphins

Dolphins love you. They come here with magical tunes, and mysteries for you. I would love to see you swim with dolphins someday and play in a new magical way.

277
Love Lasts

Love lasts forever. If you love someone and they love you — this love lasts forever. This is the love of a parent and child. It is ALWAYS available to you. This is love between sisters and brothers. Real Love has no end.

278
Hear

Listen. Hear the sounds of a bee buzzing, bluebird chirping, a lawnmower mowing, church bells ringing or a plane flying overhead. Each is AMAZING in its own way. Listen with wonder to whatever sounds are before you.

279
Beauty

Mathematicians love numbers. They believe they are beautiful. Everyone sees beauty in different places and spaces. What is beauty to you right now?

280
Horses

Horses teach us to trust ourselves! They always check in their bodies and see how they feel before going ahead. So like a horse, you can trust what messages you get from your stomach, head and heart to give you a strong start.

281
A Holy Curiosity

Being curious is a really smart way to be! It helps open your mind, and find new ways to look at things. It's that feeling when you really, really are interested in something and really, really want to know. What are you curious about today?

282
Wonder

Ever wonder about life's mysteries? Like how many stars are in the sky, and how many fish in the sea? Nobody, not you or me, knows such things. Shall we look up at the stars tonight?

283
Play Away

Play away today! Enjoy being completely free and playing to your hearts desire whether it's climbing a tree, singing to me or jumping on the trampoline to feel a big sense of Wee, Wee and Wee!

284
Imagine

Close your eyes and imagine a really beautiful place. It is full of EVERYTHING that you love, feel really good about and makes your heart happy. Look around, take in the smells and feel its beauty. When you are ready — open your eyes and tell me where you went...

285
Be the Bat

Bats fly without even seeing! Did you know that? They have a special sense that guides them, just like you have too. They trust it through and through. What special sense guides you? (i.e. feeling, thinking, physical, hearing and seeing)

286
Joy of Dirt

Dirt is extra special holding minerals and nutrients for worms, bugs and all sorts of plant life. Every beautiful flower needs dirt to live. Do you want to plant a seed in dirt, and watch it grow? You can root for it as it goes!

287
Animal Life

Every animal loves another! Big elephants wrap their trunks around their babies, bears cuddle with their cubs and squirrels squeeze together to sleep in one cozy nest. What animals have you seen loving each other?

288
Adventure

Helen Keller stated that life is either a daring adventure or nothing at all!   Are you having a daring adventure? If not, let's figure out how to dare more.

289
Crystals

Crystals make me happy! Even a little bit snappy. They are so powerful just like me and you. Maybe we can look for some soon and clean them under the moon. Like rose quartz, amethyst, jade or tigers eye...

290
Why

Why was one of my absolute favorite words! It made me wonder about life, people and how everything worked. Native Americans consider *why* as one of the most sacred words on Earth. Do ever wonder why about anything?

291
Go to Serve

Going around the world giving a helping hand makes your own heart really, really happy! You can explore places and put smiles on faces. You see, someone somewhere always can use a helping hand — where might you want to go someday and give a helping hand?

292
Silly

Bring the silly wherever you go! Up on a hill you may need extra silly-willy, or down at the beach you might even need to teach silly-dilly.   Just remember wherever you go, it's the silly parts that open hearts.

293
Kites Remind Us We Can Fly

Kites up in the sky fly oh so high! They brighten our days and make us remember lighter ways. So off they go, flying about, crashing into the sea and playing with me. Want to go fly a kite soon?

294
Magic Dreams

Dreams send magical messages from beyond time and space! Not long ago I had a dream and it came true. What have your dreams been telling you?

295
Play Together

Let's play together! We can make a puzzle, create a book with illustrations or sing a song that makes me laugh and be silly to you. Or something else totally new. What do you want to do?

296
Making It UP

Let's make it up! Each of us can be something we've always wanted to be like Fairy, Princess or Rescue Pilot. Want to do it now and play with me?

297
Got Color

Use some color today in a completely new way! Paint, draw, create or make a fun book full of your own colorful drawings that tells a story by YOU to ME for all to see.

298
Fully You

I want you to be FULLY you in everything you do! So enjoy discovering your self, taking your talents off the shelf and being fully the wonderful you. What do you fully want to do?

299
Explore More

Some places have butterflies you can feed, crystals you can mine or museums that tell great stories about rocks, crystals, animals and things you can touch. Is there something you want to explore more of?

300
Bird's Eye View

Close your eyes. Imagine you are a bird soaring in the sky. What can you see? Tell me. Does life feel completely new from a bird's eye view?

301
Make Something New

Learn how to make something completely new to you! Like a birdhouse, tire swing, apple pie, teddy bear, necklace, fort, model boat or more. What do you make completely new just for you?

302
Sound of Music

Ever sit quietly and listen fully to the sound of music? With your eyes closed, ears open and just fully 100% listening to the music. You can let it fill you up, and then experience how it brings you to a happier feeling place. Want to try?

303
Angel Meeting

Want to meet your Guardian Angel? Close your eyes and see yourself meeting your Angel. You are both together on a bench. She then sees you get really bright, and gives you a gift. What is it?

304
Turtle

Ever see a turtle? A turtle teaches us how to go slow, and arrive somewhere right on time. Turtle steps are small but wise. Take some turtle steps today that are small and wise in every way. Want to show me?

305
Special Talk

Ever talk to a bird? Are you heard? How about talking to a tree? Do you think it hears thee? See what you can do, as you move throughout your day interacting with plants and animals in a new way.

306
Tummy Knows Best

Your tummy knows best! Forget all the rest. Your tummy feels yummy when all is well and swell. It feels icky and sticky when things are bumpy and grumpy. So follow the happy tummy to feel your best.

307
Child's Pose

Learn a little yoga to help you unwind and empty your mind. It is the child's pose that is easy, and helps you repose. So let's find out more, and open the yoga door.

308
Light

Light changes everything! Look for the happy light of the morning sun, midday bright or evening gold, which is magical I am told. What type of light do you love?

309
Time Machine

If you magically had a time machine that could take you anywhere in time and space — where would you go? And why? Tell me all about it.

310
Symbols

Symbols like the peace sign, round sun, star, heart and moon are important to you. What's your favorite little symbol today?

311
Clay

Clay, play dough and cookie dough are all so much fun! You get to make something from nothing. Want to play with one soon? We could do it and listen to a cool tune.

312
Solve Something

Ever want to solve something? Like putting the pieces of puzzle together or finding where the missing socks are for your mother! Look to solve things in new ways today.

313
Discover

You are your VERY OWN explorer on this planet going where no one has gone before! What do you want to discover?

314
Species Watch

Ever watch another species or form of life? Like the birds flying together, ants building their hill or groundhogs going underground. Look for species to watch in your world and observe how they talk, walk and communicate without words...

315
Time Capsule

Ever create a time capsule? You put a few things in a box, write yourself a note and put it in a safe place. Then maybe 5 or 10 years from now you can go back and see the message you wrote to your FUTURE SELF! Want to try it?

316
Wish

Make a wish! Now is a special time for you. Angels will bring you love through and through. So close your eyes and make a wish. Now let it go and enjoy the unfolding of your show.

317
Myths

Do you know what a myth is? It's a sacred story with hidden messages... One myth is of Artemis, the goddess of forest and hills. She also helps children find their way. Learn about an Ancient Greek, Roman or other myth today.

318
Blue

Blue is a color of calm, and relaxation. It soothes the body and heals the mind. It makes you feel like clouds floating by and all is swell. Look for some blue in your world today!

319
Bell

Listen for bells today. Be them church, school or cow bells. The sound of a bell means an angel got his wings. Do you believe in angels? I sure do. Angels love to help with ANYTHING. So ask away and they'll come to your rescue today.

320
Natural

Growing up is natural! You get bigger and stronger each day. Enjoy growing up and becoming a bigger person. It just means that all your dreams will get a chance to dance. Smile and know that this is really an infinite show.

321
Mandala Coloring

Color in a mandala. A mandala is composed of sacred shapes that symbolize the whole universe. Coloring them in is fun and focuses your mind! It unleashes your creativity, and brings the whole world into your hands.

322
Circles

Circles are special shapes. Up in the sky is the round sun and under us the circular earth. Ancient Egyptians worshipped the sun. See how circles influence you. Do you love a full moon? Or bouncing ball? Or round apple?

323
Beauty

Beauty is in the eye of the beholder. See something beautiful today! Give it your attention in every way. Let it move you. It may be music that makes you shake your BOOTY or an ice cream cone that makes you feel FRUITY.

324
Extra-ordinary

Beyond the regular is the EXTRAORDINARY. It is all around us!!! Giraffes in the zoo or Polar Bears that sneeze "Hatch-Chew." Open a book to see the WONDERS of the world. They are here for you to see from sea to shining sea.

325
Colors

Learn about colors today! Mix red and blue to get purple. Add some white and it gets light. See how colors change everything. Grow your own connection to colors and how they make you feel.

326
Love

Love is like a 4-leaf clover. It feels lucky to have it! There is family love, friend love, puppy love, god love and grown-up love. Learn about GREAT stories of love today. Like the TAJ MAHAL, Mother Teresa and The Sound of Music.

327
Wishes

Aladdin was a Genie that grants three wishes!   Close your eyes and make three wishes. Don't tell anyone what you wished for today. Let them go and get on with your show.

328
Kindness

Einstein the great scientist stated that Kindness, Beauty and Truth helped him courageously face each day cheerfully. What is kindness? Can you be kind to animals? To people? To plants and the earth? Tell me about how you can be kind today.

329
Boundless

Boundless joy is for every girl and boy. It feels so free it makes your heart HAPPY. It's like climbing a mountain and getting to the top! Or taking a boat trip and you steering the way! What makes you feel happy and free today?

330
NEW

So many places exist for YOU! Hawaii has lava rocks, Mexico has ancient clocks, Holland has tulips across the hills and Tibet has ancient magical pills. All over the world are secrets and stories waiting for you to see their GLORIES.

331
Prayer Flags

Make a prayer flag. Put a name on the back of each flag and tie them together with a rope. Hang them out with great hope. Sending prayers shows the world you cares.

332
No Ordinary

There are no ordinary moments! Every second is special. Even if you are picking your nose or wiggling your toes! God is here, there and everywhere. So see the DIVINE light shining everywhere even at night.

333
Knowing

Inner knowing is where our truth is glowing. It has no words. It cannot be heard. Trust your feeling center — it will ALWAYS tell you the truth about someone, something and someplace so you can wear your happiest face.

334
Freedom

Freedom's just another word for nothing left to loose, said Janis Joplin. She was a singer who sang with all her heart. She was really FREE. Learning that you are FREE to be ANYTHING you want is a happy note. Make choices today that make you feel FREE.

335
Discovery

Discover something anew like Christopher Columbus sailing the ocean blue. Use a telescope, thermometer, microscope or some other nifty device. ENJOY finding something new that's been waiting just for you...

336
To Be

See what's not there yet but coming to be! Robert Fulton looked into a boiling pot and invented the steamboat. He let his mind imagine it to be...and soon we could all see.

337
Breathe

Breathe it out. Lift your shoulders up, roll them back and put them down with a BIG SOUND of "HUUGH" coming out of your mouth. Do it three times and let it all out. Feel the tension going out and room for joy coming in.

338
Perfect Now

You are perfectly loved right now. You don't need to prove anything to me or anyone else on this planet. You only work is to "follow your bliss" as Joseph Campbell said. Enjoy finding your bliss and happy feeling today.

339
Unfolding

Live like a river flows carried by the surprises of its unfolding, explained John O' Donohue. It means to be happy with the natural rhythm of life ~ always open to the magical occurrences on the way.

340
Live the Mystery

Every day we are asked to live the mystery. It's an enigma of where we were before life and where we go upon death! And the mystery continues each and every day as the sun amazingly sets, moon incredibly rises and earth spins on its axis. Enjoy living the mystery today.

341
Start and End

Life has a beginning and an end. All is natural and healthy. There is a time to be born, live and die. None of us know the end of our stories — so each day needs to be lived to the fullest. Go out and live this day to the fullest.

342
Stupendous

See something stupendous. Something really, really BIG like the Intrepid Boat in New York City, the Amazon River in South America or the Great Wall of China. See something that dazzles your eyes and blows your mind.

343
Sound

Sound is everywhere. At sunset cardinals chirp to find friends. Cats purr upon waking to no ends. What is your sound and what does it say? Do you make it each and every day?

344
You and God

Your life is between you and God. No one else. You came to be in a special spot only YOU can fill. No one before you and no one after you will take your place. It is a divine assignment in this time and space.

345
Lucky Charm

Make a lucky charm. It will keep away harm. You can keep it in your pocket or wear it like a locket. It may be stone, crystal or bone. It needs to feel strong as it keeps you ever-long.

346
Believe

Believe in your power. You are more AMAZING every hour. I love your spunkiness even its funkiness. So use it well and you'll always feel swell.

347
Day Tripper

Plan a real day trip soon to see something new and special to you! Maybe a baseball game where hot dogs call your name, or the opera where they sing, dance and prance. No matter the trip, big tall or small - I think it will be a real rip!

348
Learn

Delve into learning about other worlds of magic and light. Atlantis, Pleiades, Aztecs, Egyptians and Native American cultures may speak to your soul. Have fun learning more as this will open a door.

349
Night Classes

Tell me a story about your dreams at night. Do you fly and feel light? Or swim to sacred spots and feel hot? I love to know how your night classes go...

350
Animal

What animal speaks to your soul? Do you think it walks with you now? I wonder why or how? Some believe each of us has invisible animal totems that come on our path — and only special people can see them. Can you see yours?

351
Fresh Air

Let the fresh air in! Air moves around without a sound. It flows and goes. Let the fresh air move and Jophiel groove. She's a magical energy sweeper and a real keeper.

352
Space

Outer space is a place of great interest to you! It holds mystery, science, life, magic and the ability to find life on other planets. Space proves we on Earth don't know everything. Anything is really possible. Big people are discovering new things just like you do every single day!

353
Seahorse

Did you know the male seahorse gets pregnant? Then when it is time - it shoots 200+ baby seahorses out its belly button area into the sea! It is truly amazing. What is the most outrageous animal you have seen?

354
Bloom

You bloom where you are planted! Enjoy being exactly where you are today and growing in every way. Can you pretend to be a tree with your arms as leaves and feet as roots? Show me.

355
Hokey Pokey

Do the hokey pokey and turn yourself around, that's what its all about! Can you do the hokey pokey? It's a perfectly silly way to get your spirits up, body moving and heart smiling happy. Learn how to hokey pokey today.

356
Life is a Dance Floor

Some say life is a stage! I say no — it's a DANCE FLOOR. Learn how to move into the rhythm of life and keep dancing regardless of the music. You may want to sing the blues or belt out an operatic tune — whatever it may be, just keep dancing!

357
Seeds

Today's seeds are tomorrow's flowers. You can plant seeds and watch flowers rise up from the dirt. Or you can plant kind words and see all kind words spring up all around you! What type of seeds are you planting now?

358
Mommies

Stand up if you have or ever had a mommy! And say "THANK YOU MOM" and mean it in every way. Moms give us so much to help us on our way. Every being has a mommy even fishes, frogs, butterflies, puppies, bears and more! Be kind to all the mommies on earth.

359
Dream Weavers

Spiders are amazing creatures! They have magical powers. Spiders weave things together from all different dimensions. And their bodies look like a figure 8 or infinity sign showing their limitless power. How are you like a spider today?

360
Ladybug

Ladybugs are beautiful creatures that teach us about our wishes! If you see a ladybug it is a lucky sign that your wishes are coming true faster than you know and all you need to do is — KEEP WISHING.

361
Bluebirds

Bluebirds symbolize happiness! If you see a bluebird fly into your life, it is reminding you that your NATURAL state is happy. Look for ways to be happy today.

362
Moon

Not long ago a man went up in rocket ship to the moon!
It was one of the most amazing things. What is amazing
to you?

363
Drum Circle

Ever play the drums together with others? It can be
so much fun! It's called a drum circle. It holds special
magic that connects us to our natural rhythms and
beating of our own hearts. Give it a start ...

364
Roots and Wings

Trees have such incredible roots bending, twisting and
curling to hold onto Mother Earth! It's a beautiful way
to hold on to Earth and then with branches reach up to
touch the sky, way up high. Can you stand like a tree for
me?

365
Imagine

Imagine all the people living life in peace said singer,
John Lennon. All the birds of the sky, fishes in the
waters, animals on the land and magical beings in space
all smiling together. Close your eyes and imagine this
feeling everywhere.

Sayings that "click" for us

Sayings that "click" for us

Sayings that "click" for us

Additional Resources

Child Development

Your Child's Growing Mind, by Jane M. Healy, Ph.D. New York: Broadway Books, 1987.

Positive Parenting

calm and compassionate children, by Susan Usha Dermond. Berkley, CA: Ten Speed Press, 2007.

the childhood roots of adult happiness, by Edward M. Hallowell, MD. New York: Ballatine Books, 2002.

How to Behave So Your Children Will, Too!, by Sal Severe, PhD. New York: Penguin Books, 2000.

Teaching Kids to Care, by Lehman, Youngs, Wafer & Wolf. New York: Hampton Roads Publishing, 2007.

Your Child's Strengths: Discover them, develop them, use them, by Jennifer Fox, M.Ed. New York: Penguin Group, 2008.

Buddhism

The Four Noble Truths: Fundamentals of the Buddhist Teachings, by His Holiness the XIV Dalai Lama. New Delhi, India: HarperCollins Publishers India, 1998.

How to See Yourself As You Really Are, by His Holiness the XIV Dalai Lama. New York: Atria Books, 2006.

Awakening the Buddha Within: Tibetan Wisdom for the Western World, by Lama Surya Das. New York: Broadway Books, 1997.

About the Author

Maureen Healy is the Founder of Growing Happy Kids, a worldwide organization focused upon fostering happiness in children. More information: www.growinghappykids.com

Healy is not new to traveling the globe and affecting positive change in children's lives. In 2007, she worked with Tibetan refugee children in India and also built child-centered programs around the United States. She has a completely unique approach that integrates the best of Eastern and Western thought.

Other notable items include being named a "Creative Activist" by Creative Visions Foundation for her play therapy toolkit for traumatized children and authoring a "Peace Curriculum" for preschoolers that is now distributed worldwide by The Simha Foundation.

Maureen's academic credentials include but are not limited to a Bachelor of Arts in Psychology and Master of Business Administration from Clark University as well as a Master of Arts program in Clinical Psychology from Fielding Graduate University. Her writing contributions include a regular Blog online at Psychology Today titled "Creative Development" as well as being the featured child expert at Pure Inspiration magazine.

.

Dedication

May all children be free from *suffering and the*
causes of *suffering.* *May all* children be happy.